This book belongs to:

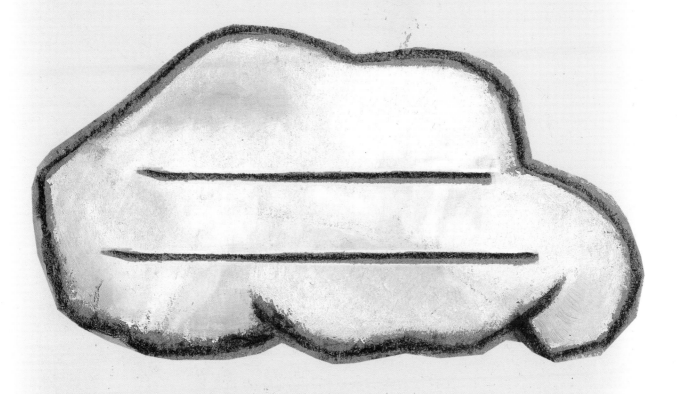

For my little Else.
A kiss from your giant - C.N.

Text copyright © 2004 Carl Norac
Illustrations copyright © 2004 Ingrid Godon
Moral rights asserted
Dual language copyright © 2004 Mantra Lingua
All rights reserved
A CIP record for this book is available
from the British Library.

First published in 2004 by Macmillan Children's Books, London
First dual language publication in 2004 by Mantra Lingua

mantra
5 Alexandra Grove, London N12 8NU
www.mantralingua.com

CARL NORAC
INGRID GODON

Mi papá es un gigante
My Daddy is a Giant

Spanish translation by Maria Helena Thomas

mantra

Mi papá es un gigante.
Cuando quiero abrazarle tengo
que subirme a una escalera.

My daddy is a giant.
When I want to cuddle him,
I have to climb a ladder.

Cuando jugamos al escondite,
mi papá tiene que esconderse
detrás de una montaña.

When we play hide-and-seek,
my daddy has to hide
behind a mountain.

Y cuando las nubes
están cansadas,
hacen una siesta sobre
los hombros de mi papá.

And when the clouds are tired,
they come and sleep
on my daddy's shoulders.

Cuando mi papá estornuda,
es como un huracán que
arrasa con el mar.

When my daddy sneezes,
it's like a hurricane.
It blows the sea away.

Cuando mi papá se ríe,
es como otro huracán que
arranca las hojas de los árboles.

When my daddy laughs,
it's like another hurricane.
All the leaves fly off the trees.

A los pájaros les
encanta mi papá.
Hacen nidos en su pelo.

Birds love my daddy.
They make their nests
in his hair.

Cuando jugamos al fútbol,
mi papá siempre gana.
Puede dar patadas que hacen
que el balón llegue a la luna.

When we play football,
my daddy always wins.

He can kick the ball as high as the moon.

Pero yo siempre gano cuando
jugamos a las canicas.
Sus dedos son
demasiado grandes.

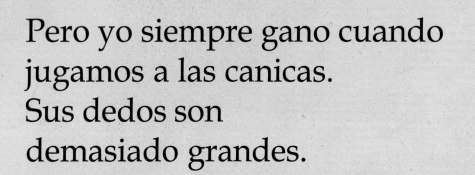

But I always beat
him at marbles.
His fingers are
far too big.

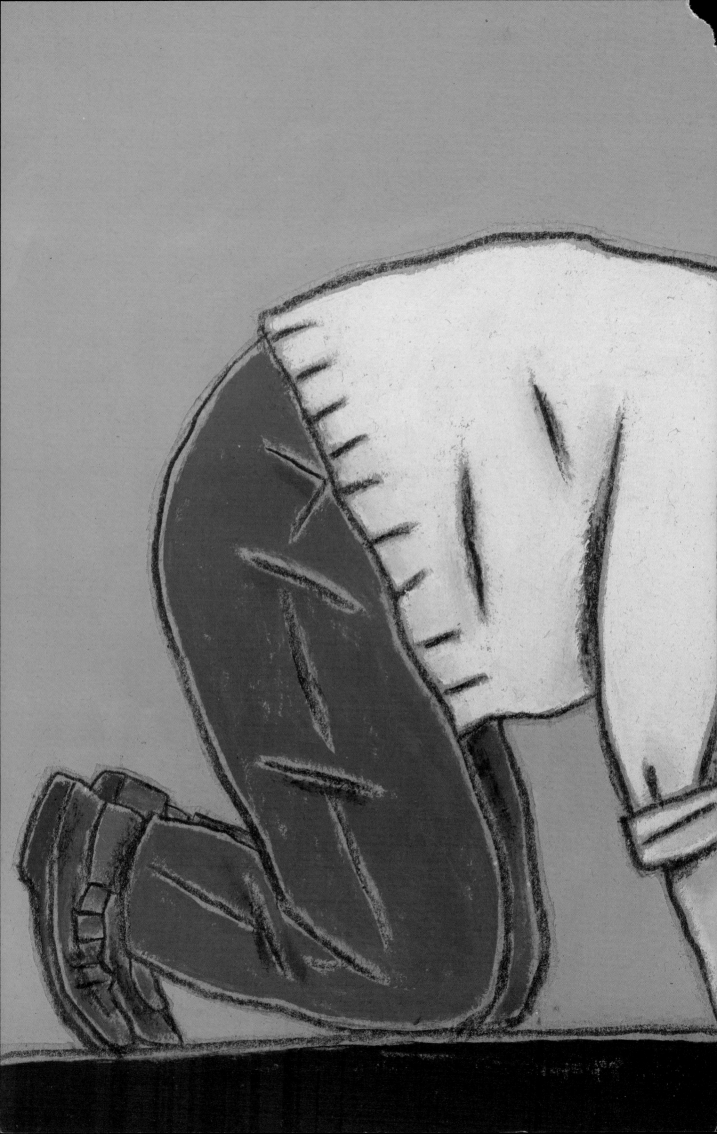

Me gusta cuando mi papá dice:
"¡Vas a ser tan alto como yo!"

I like it when my
daddy says,
"You're getting as
tall as me!"

Cuando mi papá corre,
la tierra tiembla como si
estuviera asustada.

When my daddy runs,

the ground shakes

as if it was scared.

Pero yo no le tengo miedo
a nada cuando estoy en los
brazos de mi papá.

But I'm not scared
of anything when
I'm in my daddy's arms.

Mi papá es un gigante,
y me quiere con su
gigante corazón.

My daddy is a giant,
and he loves me with
all his giant heart.

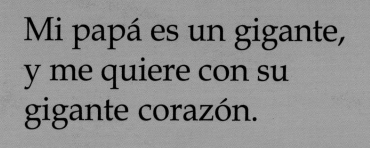